Royal Deeside,
Grampian Highlands and Aberueen

Photography by Colin Baxter

Text by Gilbert Summers

Colin Baxter Photography Limited, Grantown-on-Spey, Scotland

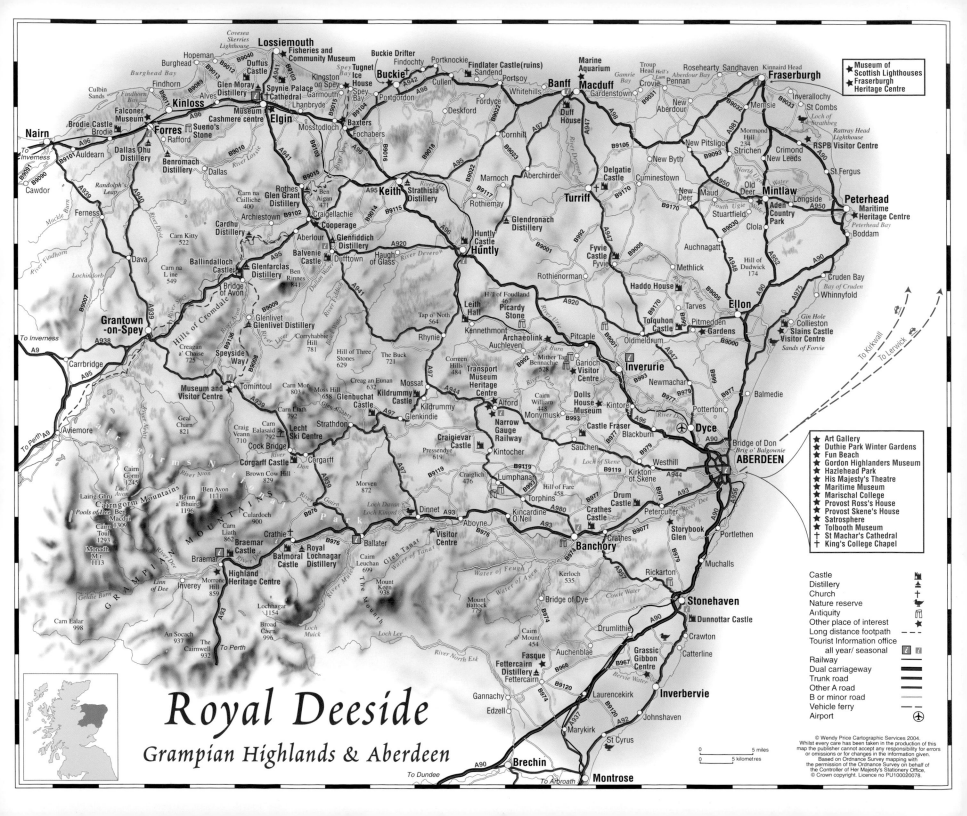

Royal Deeside
Grampian Highlands & Aberdeen

Legend / Key:

- ★ Museum of Scottish Lighthouses
- ★ Fraserburgh Heritage Centre

- ★ Art Gallery
- ♣ Duthie Park Winter Gardens
- ★ Fun Beach
- ★ Gordon Highlanders Museum
- ★ Hazlehead Park
- ★ His Majesty's Theatre
- ★ Maritime Museum
- ★ Marischal College
- ★ Provost Ross's House
- ★ Provost Skene's House
- ★ Satrosphere
- ★ Tolbooth Museum
- † St Machar's Cathedral
- † King's College Chapel

- 🏰 Castle
- ⚒ Distillery
- † Church
- Nature reserve
- 🏛 Antiquity
- ★ Other place of interest
- – – – Long distance footpath
- 🛈 Tourist Information office — all year/ seasonal
- Railway
- Dual carriageway
- Trunk road
- Other A road
- B or minor road
- Vehicle ferry
- ✈ Airport

0   5 miles
0   5 kilometres

Royal Deeside,
Grampian Highlands and Aberdeen

CONTENTS

Royal Deeside & Grampian Highlands

Introduction

The big wedge of Scotland, sometimes known as Grampian, widens out from the heart of the Cairngorms and takes in both the east-facing North Sea coast and the Moray Firth from its turning point at Kinnaird Head on the north-eastern tip. It includes some of Scotland's grandest mountains, and also wild coastline. Inland from these hardly discovered seascapes, an intensively farmed coastal strip gradually gives way to moors, woodland and hills. These are the outliers of the highest part of the Grampian mountains, called the Cairngorms. The area's main rivers also flow north and east, adding to the scenic variety.

This corner of Scotland is called a variety of names: 'the land at the bend in the ocean', for example. This is a reference to Kinnaird Head again, thought to be the Promontorium Taezalum that appears on the ancient Egyptian cartographer Ptolemy's world map. This names the Taizali, a Pictish tribe who once inhabited the far north-east and confronted the Romans in their brief northern adventures in AD 83. More recently, the north-east of Scotland has sometimes been described as the 'Grampian cocoon'. The name suggests two things. Firstly, that in former times the north-east lay out of the mainstream of turbulent Scottish history: few great battles were fought here, neither was the area the setting for many events that shaped the nation of Scotland. Secondly, it implies that the area has been almost asleep, untouched and unchanged, or at the very least self-sufficient and independent from other parts of Scotland.

This notion of self-sufficiency originally sprang from the very real geographical barrier of the Grampian mountains themselves. Scotland's north-east was for centuries literally beyond the mountains. The Grampian massif runs down almost to the sea by Stonehaven, cut off sharply by what geologists call the Highland Boundary Fault, running diagonally (i.e. to the north-east) from Perthshire and Angus. No coincidence therefore that at the very end of the Dark Ages, it was the Pictish 'mormaors', or leaders, of the relatively isolated north-east who were the last to stand against the changing order of ninth- and tenth-century Scotland, with the Scots themselves expanding from their western power-bases. (See Sueno's Stone in the Moray section, p.61.)

The high-ground barrier between Lowland and Highland hereabouts is known as 'The Mounth' (from Gaelic 'monadh', meaning moor). Cutting into the high plateau are steep-sided glens, especially on the Angus side, from the head of which run ancient through-routes which eventually drop into the valley of the River Dee. The best known of these, because the main A93 road uses it, comes over the high pass of Glenshee, overlooked by the rounded high top of the Cairnwell, to reach Braemar. It is these high-level entry routes to the northlands that gave rise to the notion of a land set apart.

Small wonder, for example, that Grampian is still the

FARMLAND, STRATHDON (opposite). Unlike the poor acid soils of Deeside, the River Don flows through richer country, where farming is an important part of the rural economy.

FISHING BOATS, PETERHEAD HARBOUR
Though quotas restrict the catch of the modern fleet, the landings at Peterhead still bring great wealth to the town, both for the crews and the processing industries.

quayside, school playground, shop or workplace, in spite of the efforts of generations of school-teachers to discourage it. It adds a richness to the linguistic landscape. Its borrowings from French, Scandinavian, Dutch and German are a reminder that the Grampian cocoon has always been very much in the eyes of the outsider, and that in common with other east-coast communities, in medieval times and beyond, there were strong trading links across the North Sea to Scandinavia, the Baltic ports and the Low Countries.

Grampian today is as forward-looking and linked-up as any other part of Scotland. This has at least something to do with, for example, its main city's involvement in the oil industry since the early 1970s.

stronghold of the Scots language. This was originally a form of Northern English that supplanted Gaelic from around the end of the thirteenth century onwards. Later, elocutionists and language purists were to label it 'Doric'. The Dorians were originally a country-dwelling tribe who lived outside ancient Athens, where 'proper' Greek was spoken. The Dorians were, in effect, seen as country bumpkins who could not speak properly – hence the term is really quite insulting to native Grampian people.

However, Doric, or braid (broad) Scots, in all its diversity can still be heard, rich or dilute, in farm,

Aberdeen was certainly changed by its role as European oil capital, while the harbour of refuge at Peterhead also had a new role to play as a service base.

Fishing remains an important part of the region's economy. As fishing vessels became ever larger and more sophisticated in their catching techniques, so there came about a decline of smaller ports and a concentration on a few large ones. Peterhead is the largest white fish landing port in Europe, while Fraserburgh claims the distinction of having the largest fishing fleet in Britain in terms of its numbers of registered vessels (over 100 in 2003). The sights, sounds and smells of a large fishing port are very much a part of the Grampian experience.

Farming is still a major influence on the look of the land. Except for the highest tops, or on dune, cliff and coastal heath, Grampian is a man-made landscape (in common with the rest of Scotland – only more obviously). The far north-east is known as Buchan, possibly related to 'bo', Gaelic for cow, and the coastal strip is important cattle-rearing country, where summer sees the pasture, hayfield and silage crops for winter feed vary from vivid emerald to a bleached yellow after a cut. The landscape also colours up with ripening barley both as feedstuff and also for malting to supply the area's native whisky distilling. The farmlands change their hue almost weekly throughout the growing season, before ploughing turns them brown and bare.

Woodland becomes more prevalent in the western part of the area, with the old county of Banffshire as a link between the bleak shoulders of Buchan to the east and the more lush and sylvan Moray. Overall, in its Cairngorm heartlands, with the boundary of Aberdeenshire running through more 4000 ft (1219 m) high mountains than any other boundary in Britain, and with the coast boasting some of the grandest cliffs in mainland Scotland, the north-east certainly offers great contrasts.

As for its built heritage, the older parts of the main towns and villages, for the most part, follow the Scottish tradition of building in solid local stonework wherever available – hence the silver granite of Aberdeen, the pinky-orange granite of Peterhead or Banchory, the red sandstone of the older parts of Turriff – and everywhere

the mauve and grey of slated roofs (some of it, at least, coming from local quarries such as the old workings at the Glens of Foudland south-east of Huntly on today's A96). The old Grampian towns and villages seem almost to grow out of the native rock.

Somewhere in this diversity of landscape and townscape, farming and fishing, wild mountain and empty coast, is a sense of something cautious and genuine, of a land without pretension. The generations of toil of its working farmers have left their mark in the drystone walls edging the fields, each stone wrestled out of the heavy clay ground. The struggle to win a living from the sea is symbolised by the old fishers' houses, built gable-end to the shore, as if defying the wind and tide. Landscape and people are intertwined here as in no other part of Scotland.

UPPER GLEN DEE

Glen Dee captures the atmosphere of the wildness of the Cairngorms – but is just one of many glens, U-shaped in profile and created by glaciation, which cut deeply into the granite plateau.

Aberdeen City

Unique in elegant silver and grey, the townscape of Aberdeen owes everything to the characteristics of its local granite: tough, resistant, with a high mica content which turns the stone face into millions of tiny mirrors in sunshine. Though the city shape as it is seen today owes much to the wave of improvement which swept through it from the end of the eighteenth century onwards, the settlement itself goes much further back. Aberdeen became a Royal Burgh – a community with trading rights paying its dues to the king – in the thirteenth century.

As the market centre for a large rural hinterland and also an old-established seaport, Aberdeen has always been a trading place, at one time exporting large quantities of woollen stockings (of all things) to the Low Countries. Later, trade diversified into other types of cloth, notably linen, by the late eighteenth century. Granite became an export around this time. Before the end of the nineteenth century, Aberdeen had a reputation for shipbuilding, particularly for the style of sailing ship known as the Aberdeen clipper, built especially for the China tea trade. Likewise around this time, Aberdeen invested heavily in its trawler fleet, with a deep-water fishery lasting well into the twentieth century.

Today, Aberdeen is Scotland's third-largest city, but still operates as a large market town for its hinterland, as can be seen by the bustle of a Saturday afternoon around the city centre. Generations of country-dwellers, and those from the towns round about, come to the city for its shopping and entertainment. In spite of oil, Aberdeen's ambience still remains essentially

maritime. Gulls with wings the colour of the local granite call overhead, and the smell of the sea is at every street corner in downtown Aberdeen. Perceived by some as a long way from Scotland's central belt, Aberdeen once advertised itself as Scotland's largest seaside resort. Today, the changing demands of holiday-makers mean that Aberdeen's extensive beach has had to re-invent itself. The traditional cafes are still there, though the seaside donkeys have long gone. In their place is a string of places of entertainment, from sports centres to nightclubs and a permanent fun fair.

The Aberdeen of today has also come about by the growing together of two separate villages. The other community, Old Aberdeen, grew up close to the River Don to the north, in a loose parallel with the developments around today's Castlegate and harbour

ABERDEEN HARBOUR (above). All kinds of vessels have anchored here; traders from the Low Countries and the Baltic, steam drifters and trawlers, fast tea clippers, and now oil rig support vessels.

UNION STREET, ABERDEEN (opposite). 'One of the finest streets in the Empire' – from the Imperial Gazetteer, *1865.*

9

**ABERDEEN –
CITY AND
HARBOUR**
*Though owing its
original wealth to the
trade through its port,
Aberdeen's long sweep
of golden sand helped
establish the city as a
holiday resort – in the
old days of traditional
beach holidays.*

at the mouth of the River Dee. Old Aberdeen was formerly called Aberdon – the mouth of the River Don. (To complicate matters, an early spelling of Aberdeen was Aberden, suggesting that the southern settlement was around the Denburn, a stream flowing through the city between the two major rivers, rather than a reference to the River Dee.)

Many historic buildings survive in Old Aberdeen which, like its southern neighbour, has interwoven strands of both a religious and an academic story. A certain St Machar was sent, it was said, by St Columba to found a church at a site described as a grassy platform where a river flowed in the shape of a shepherd's crook. The river was the Don, and the site became St Machar's Cathedral in Old Aberdeen.

This first church of St Machar was built around AD 580, though nothing now remains of the original foundation. As it stands today, the exact dating of some of the cathedral work is quite complex. Its nave was rebuilt in red sandstone around 1370, with granite finishing the work by the mid fifteenth century. The twin octagonal spires date from the first half of the sixteenth century. The Bishopric here was founded by King David I who moved it from Mortlach in Dufftown, Moray, another ancient religious site. From the cathedral, there is a fine view over the winding Don, and Seaton Park below, particularly fine in spring with its drifts of daffodils, or in high summer when the herbaceous plantings are full of colour.

At the far end of the park from the cathedral, the Don flows under the picturesque Brig o' Balgownie. Until 1827, this was the only road out of Aberdeen to the north. Remarkably, the structure dates from around

1314 when it was built by Richard Cementarius, who was Aberdeen's first provost (Scots for mayor).

In the other direction from the cathedral, the Chanonry (i.e. the street of the canons) leads southwards with the excellent and sometimes overlooked Cruickshank Botanic Gardens on one side. After crossing St Machar Drive, the inner ring road that cuts through this area, the main route becomes the High Street. This runs south from the Town House of Old Aberdeen, a classical Georgian design of 1788, via university properties to the campus of King's College, instantly recognisable by the crown spire adorning King's College Chapel. The College itself was founded in 1494, with the handsome spire dating from 1500. Within the Chapel is a tall oak screen separating nave and choir, which, along with the ribbed wooden ceiling and stalls, is acclaimed as the finest late-medieval wood carving in all of Scotland. Taken altogether, there is plenty of atmosphere in Old Aberdeen, bustling with students in term time, with a backdrop of fine buildings to set the scene. Today, urban expansion has joined Old Aberdeen to the main part of the city.

The oldest part of downtown Aberdeen, around the Castlegate, the original market place, lost its castle long ago. This was sited somewhere behind the dominating baronial granite tower which today ends the view down Union Street, the main street. This grand tower belongs to the Salvation Army Citadel of 1896, the design of which was inspired by Balmoral Castle.

The market cross, the very symbol of a Scottish burgh, can also be seen here. Dating from 1686, its 12 panels above the arcades carry portraits of the Stuart monarchs and the arms of the city. Nearby, the city's seventeenth-century tolbooth, (or town house) the place of justice and administration in old Scottish burghs, today offers visitors tours of its cells.

St Nicholas Kirk is the oldest church in Aberdeen, the original 'Mither Kirk'. It was founded before 1151 and at that time lay to the east of the settlement. The oldest parts are the pillars, which support a much later tower. Its clerestory windows date from the original twelfth-century building. St Nicholas Kirk was divided into East and West Kirks at the Reformation and there was much rebuilding from 1741 onwards. The kirkyard with its table tombs is a comparatively peaceful spot, much frequented by shoppers and office workers, especially in warm weather.

As in Old Aberdeen, this part of the city also has a

KING'S COLLEGE CHAPEL.
The crown spire of the chapel was blown down in 1633 but later rebuilt.

COAT OF ARMS, Marischal College.

ABERDEEN Town House, Clock Tower

famous and instantly recognisable university building. Marischal College was founded by the Earl Marischal in 1593 as a Protestant alternative to the Catholic King's College. (Earl Marischal is a hereditary office and means the keeper of the king's mares.) Though, architecturally speaking, tough granite is usually associated with heavy, massive effects, the extraordinary facade of Marischal College uses the stone like cake-decoration, achieving a light and graceful result which is technically quite remarkable. The design dates from 1891 and, when finished, created the second-largest granite building in the world, only El Escorial in Spain being larger.

Another place to view granite and its many shades is within the portals of Aberdeen Art Gallery. Worth visiting on its own account, with a particularly fine watercolour section, in addition the main hallway of the building is lined with polished granite pillars, no two alike, having been quarried in different parts of Europe – in pink, grey, orange and almost black. The Gallery is only moments from another of the city's landmarks – the juxtaposition of the main library, St Mark's Church, and His Majesty's Theatre. Library and church date from the end of the nineteenth century, the theatre slightly later (its interior now restored to full Edwardian splendour). Aberdonians have for long referred to the grouping as 'Education, Salvation and Damnation'.

Aberdeen is definitely a city for exploring on foot. Most of the interesting buildings are in the commercial centre around Union Street. This main street was the architectural means by which the growing city escaped from its eastern confines in 1801. It marched away to the west in a series of soundly designed building schemes carried out over the next hundred years, so that for generations of folk from the north-east, this street was the commercial and shopping heart of the city. The late twentieth-century predilection for covered shopping malls (which the wealthy city and its comfortably-off hinterland supports enthusiastically) has disturbed this arrangement a little, but Union Street is still the axis round which the city revolves.

The city's involvement with the sea is told in the Maritime Museum, housed in part in Provost Ross's House of 1593 and built on the Shiprow, a very old street leading down to the first harbour. Even earlier – 1545 – is the date associated with Provost Skene's House. Steeply gabled and rubble-built, this ancient structure is tucked away almost beneath the concrete supports of the modern construction of St Nicholas House. Once it was a domestic dwelling in an area of similar, closely packed houses. Now it stands amid the concrete of the twentieth century as a museum of civic life, complete with restored, furnished, period rooms and early painted ceilings.

With another museum of major importance housed in Marischal College opposite, the city has a good record of its heritage. Though the past is acknowledged, the city will strike the first-time visitor as a vibrant go-ahead kind of place. The prosperity of both the oil developments of the last two decades, plus the wealth of its rural hinterland, supports a good array of shops, pubs, restaurants, places of entertainment, and a wide-ranging cultural and artistic life. Aberdeen is not some far-flung northern outpost – but is certainly different from other British cities.

MARISCHAL COLLEGE
The original Marischal College was founded in the redundant Greyfriars Monastery near today's Broad Street. Marischal College joined with King's to form Aberdeen University in 1860.

Kincardine & Deeside

This is the most mountainous part of Grampian and takes in the lands around the River Dee, as well as the old county of Kincardine, which had Stonehaven as its chief administrative town. Now all this area comes under the unitary authority of Aberdeenshire, which in its western portion takes the line of the old county boundary running far into the Cairngorms. The Pools of Dee, the very source of the River Dee, lie high on the ancient mountain through-route of the Lairig Ghru. This links the valleys of the River Dee with the River Spey, and traverses the bare block-fields and scanty wind-scoured mosses of the Cairngorm heartlands.

This wildest, highest portion of Grampian is best explored on foot. The main A93 road turns at Braemar to seek a southern way through the mountain barrier, while a minor public road goes only as far west as the Linn of Dee beyond Inverey. This cul-de-sac road returns eastwards a short way by the north bank of the River Dee. However, not all the scenic places hereabouts demand a long walk into the mountains. For example, the road-end beyond the Linn o' Dee is the starting point for a short walk to 'The Devil's Punch Bowl'. In the pinewood, the Quoich Water swirls over rocks where loose boulders have carved out and polished numerous hollows and pots.

Equally spectacular is the Linn of Dee itself, where the waters roar through a narrow channel, and where tree-roots and smoothed grey granite mean visitors should take care. Look for salmon in the gentler pools below the narrows. You can also see these fish at another spectacular rocky place nearby, 'The Colonel's Bed', in Glen Ey due south of the hamlet of Inverey.

Well hidden on the moor, but close to the main path, this rocky chasm is associated with Colonel John Farquharson who, tradition relates, was on the side of the Jacobites at Killiecrankie (1689) but later took refuge in the narrow gorge, on a ledge just above the water of the Ey Burn. These are just some of the shorter expeditions, though there are many longer ones for fit walkers by way of Glen Lui and Glen Derry into the silent space of the big hills.

The village of Braemar has a pleasant, pine-scented, almost alpine air, especially in winter, and makes a good walking centre. Routes include a fairly challenging walk to the top of Morrone Hill, 2818 ft (859 m) above the village. At the hill's lower level there is a fine birchwood and national nature reserve. In the village, the Braemar Heritage Centre tells the story of the community here, particularly its association with the Braemar Highland Gathering and its part in the royal family's connection with the area. Far back in time, Braemar was a hunting resort of the Scottish

CAIRNGORMS AND UPPER DEE from Morrone Hill (opposite). Looking west from high above Braemar to the granite heartlands of Aberdeenshire.

BRAEMAR HIGHLAND GAMES (below). With its massed pipe bands and its annual royal presence, this is perhaps the most famous of Scotland's Highland Gatherings.

**LOCHNAGAR
AND BALMORAL**
*The woodlands of
Deeside bring many
visitors to the area.
Balmoral Castle lies
just south of the River
Dee, while in the
distance, the peak
of Lochnagar marks
the northern edge of
the Mounth plateau.*

monarchs, though the royal castle of Kindrochit is little
more than a ruined shell.

Braemar Castle itself (1628) can be visited to the
east of the village. This tower house has a star-shaped
defensive wall, added when it garrisoned government
troops after the last Jacobite uprising in 1745. The
village is also closely associated with an earlier Jacobite
uprising in 1715, when the 'Braes o' Mar' was the Earl
of Mar's rallying point as leader of the rebellion against
the Hanoverian government.

Further east is the Old Bridge of Invercauld, which

formerly carried the old military road from Glenshee
and the south, en route for Fort George. Now the
bridge is one of the most recognisable of Grampian
images, with the foothills of Lochnagar behind.
Dominating southerly views from the stretch of the
Dee valley, the scale of Lochnagar can best be
appreciated from the B976 – still on the route of the
former military road – which runs north from Crathie
by Balmoral Castle. This switchback road offers fine
views southwards over the Lochnagar massif, just a mile
or so from the main Deeside road, and, from the road's

summit a mile or so further on, a westward panorama of silent whaleback hills on the eastern edge of the Cairngorms.

Many visitors in this part of Deeside go to Balmoral Castle, though only the grounds and the ballroom are open for some of the main season. (The high security on the estate means that at other times, a visitor attempting a quick look will not get very far!) The royal family's association with Deeside goes as far back as 1842 when a chance remark was made by Queen Victoria's doctor about his son, who had been on Deeside in glorious sunshine. During the same period, the Queen had been in the west (near Loch Laggan) under a continuous downpour! Soon afterwards, the lease for the old castle at Balmoral came up. By 1855 Prince Albert had bought the Balmoral estate and built a new castle, which has been in continuous use ever since, as an escape for the royals from the cares of office.

At all times of year you can stroll down from the tourist information centre at Balmoral to see the kirkyard containing the grave of John Brown, Victoria's faithful retainer, or visit the Royal Lochnagar Distillery. (Note that 'royal' attaches itself to many places in the vicinity!)

As for Lochnagar itself, it may be approached from the old pinewood, the Ballochbuie, to the west, though the most popular route to this spectacular hill is from the end of the public road at Glen Muick. One of Scotland's most popular Munros (mountains over 3000 ft high), at 3786 ft (1155 m) Lochnagar's ascent should not be undertaken lightly and is essentially a whole day expedition. Even to walk as far as the view down to the hill's impressive corrie-loch, flanked by

BALMORAL CASTLE
In 1852, Prince Albert paid 30,000 guineas for the 17,400 acres (7042 hectares) called the Balmoral Estate. The present Balmoral Castle was built thereafter, close to the site of the original.

LOCH MUICK
Though half-hidden
in its glacial trough,
Loch Muick is less
of a secret today.
Queen Victoria built
the Glas-allt Shiel
at its far end, as a
small hideaway house.

This well-laid-out little town owes its existence directly to the building of a bridge across the Dee here in 1783. This was necessary because of the popularity of the supposed healing waters of the Pannanich Wells, opposite the hamlet of Tulloch, a mile or so east of Ballater, first publicised in 1760. The 'Lourdes of Deeside' attracted visitors thereafter. The bare moor beyond the bridge on the north side was bought by speculators and laid out as Ballater, in order to cater for the tourists.

Today, the original bridge has been replaced by the (inevitably) Royal Bridge, opened by Queen Victoria, and many of the shops of the town, from the bakers' to the country-clothing stores display their 'By Royal Appointment' signs.

awesome grey cliffs, demands a good level of fitness.

Beyond the road-end in Glen Muick lie the deep, dour reaches of Loch Muick, with steep, dark hillslopes plunging down into grey waters. Long-distance paths run on both sides, going far into the Grampian tops. Near the Glen Muick road-end the high Capel Mounth track drops into the glen. The Mounth routes across the tundra-plateau of the high Grampian tops are ancient rights-of-way, linking the head of the Angus glens with those in Aberdeenshire.

Glen Muick, which has a fine waterfall in its lower reaches, runs back to the main valley close to Ballater.

Continuing downstream, the birchwoods of Deeside are at their best on the Muir of Dinnet. On this glacial hollow lie Lochs Kinord and Davan, both 'kettle-holes' – lochs in areas where giant ice blocks, left by the retreating glaciers, have melted. Among the choice of walks here, a signed walkway leads to the Burn o' Vat, a curious hollow hemmed in by rock walls, another glacial meltwater feature. Wildlife here includes good flights of overwintering geese on the lochs, and otters too. Amongst the flora, bearberry, with its red berries in autumn, is conspicuous among the lush heather. North of the nature reserve and above Logie Coldstone, the main A97 offers a fine prospect southwards over the extensively wooded glacial plain surrounded by high hills, of which Mount Keen is the most prominent.

Crossing the Dee by the bridge at Dinnet and taking the south Deeside road (the B976), is the best approach to Glen Tanar. Here the Mounth track known as the Firmounth comes down from the high ground, while the Mounth Road lies in the glen itself. The Mounth Road passes to the west side of Mount Keen, at 3081 ft (939 m), Scotland's most easterly Munro. Glen Tanar is well worth visiting, not only for the interpretative information on the estate's own visitor centre but for some fine pinewoods, with some natural regeneration, notably to the south of the Water of Tanar. Some of the mature trees here are said to be more than 250 years old. The rare capercaillie, the big grouse of the pinewoods, still occurs here, along with other Scottish specialities such as crossbills. Like the Muir of Dinnet, Glen Tanar is also looked after by Scottish Natural Heritage.

The village of Aboyne is a few minutes drive away. Like many other north-east communities, this is another planned village, its layout mostly the work of the Manchester banker, Sir William Cunliffe Brooks, who owned Glentanar estate as well. There was a settlement in existence here before the hand of the improving landlord made its mark, as the village had Royal Burgh status from 1676. Like Braemar to the west, Aboyne is noted for its annual Highland Games.

To the north is the pleasantly quiet country village of Tarland, while to the east is Lumphanan. Still primarily an agricultural area, the long continuity of settlement here is suggested by the various prehistoric sites, including stone circles, and a souterrain, the Culsh Earth House (off the B9119 north of Aboyne). This subterranean monument was used as a store, presumably for agricultural produce, about 3000 years ago. Lumphanan is associated with the end of the famous King Macbeth, killed by King Malcolm III (the famous Canmore) in battle in the woods nearby in 1057. A cairn marks the likely spot. Also very near is one of Grampian's earliest medieval earthworks, the Peel of Lumphanan, an impressive mound dating from the thirteenth century.

Back in the river valley, nearby Kincardine o' Neil straddles the main road. Though a small village, it is one of the oldest settlements on Deeside, formerly on an important crossroads where east-west traffic met travellers from the south, who (having traversed the Mounth) could ford the River Dee safely here. Some

CAMBUS O' MAY
SUSPENSION
BRIDGE
This Victorian bridge takes its name from the Gaelic meaning 'the bend of the plain'.

Potarch is associated with the Highland tradition of 'clach cuid fir' or 'manhood stones', where lifting stones is used as a test of strength. The Potarch stones or the 'Stones of Dee' reside at the hotel by the Bridge of Potarch. The pair of stones have rings set into them (and at one time travellers tied their horses to them). They are associated with the famous old-time Highland Games athlete Donald Dinnie (1837-1916). He lifted them and carried them more than once, hence their other name of the Dinnie Steens.

Potarch is just a few minutes by road from Banchory, a handsome little town in locally quarried pink granite. Also well within the commuter belt of Aberdeen, Banchory has traditionally attracted day trippers from the city on leisurely Sunday drives. The popularity of Deeside as a result of royal involvement made Banchory something of a resort and tourist gateway town from Victorian times onwards. The Brig o' Feugh is one of the places popular with visitors to the town, just above where the north-flowing Water of Feugh joins the River Dee. The tree-shaded white-water falls on the river are noted for their leaping salmon. A special pedestrian

ABOYNE AND THE RIVER DEE
From the Gaelic meaning 'the place of rippling waters', Aboyne is a popular Deeside destination, as well as a centre for some of Scotland's finest river angling.

associate the place with the army of occupation of King Edward I, who is said to have passed this way. The village's antiquity is suggested by the Norman work on the ruined church, built around 1233 as a hospice for Mounth travellers. The village later became an important market place and also a drovers' stance in the days when great herds of cattle from the north-east would be driven south to markets at Crieff or Falkirk.

Eastwards at Potarch, yet another of the Dee's scenic bridges marks where the old military road coming over the Cairn o' Mount reaches the river.

walkway spans the cataract, to make viewing easier.

Close to Banchory to the east is Crathes Castle, one of the most famous of Grampian's grand houses in the care of the National Trust for Scotland. This sixteenth-century tower house was built by the Burnett family and occupied continuously by them until the 1950s. As well as original furniture, the building is noted for its early painted ceilings and – perhaps, inevitably – the castle ghost, a green lady. In the castle policies (Scots for grounds) equally famous gardens are laid out, divided into eight 'rooms', each with a different theme. Together, castle and grounds are one of the most popular attractions anywhere in the north-east.

Also within easy reach is Drum Castle. It stands in the centre of the old grounds of Park and Drumoak, in medieval times a hunting forest of the Scottish monarchs. The original keep of Drum was given to William de Irwin by King Robert I (the Bruce) in 1323. It is said the rounded corners of the tower, with walls up to 12 ft (3.6 m) thick, were designed to make attack by battering ram more difficult. This massive square tower remained in the hands of his descendants, the Irvines, for the next 653 years. A seventeenth-century mansion was added to the original tower. Apart from some Victorian re-modelling, the original building retains much of the atmosphere of a medieval keep. Like Crathes, Drum is also in the care of the National Trust for Scotland.

To the south, two of the old rights of way are motorable roads. The first of these is the famous Cairn o' Mount road, the B974 between Banchory and Fettercairn, notable for its winter snowfalls. At the summit of the road is the Cairn itself, around 1490 ft (455 m) above sea level. Dating from the early part

of the second millennium BC, this is a fairly typical example of the summit or skyline cairns of Grampian. Because of its location as an ancient landmark, the shape of the cairn has been altered by additions made by generations of travellers. From all around there are magnificent views, particularly southwards, out of Grampian and over Angus as far as the Lomond Hills of Fife. It is a particularly atmospheric place in autumn when (as in Glen Muick, for example) the bellowing of rutting stags adds a wild sound to the upland scene.

The B974 descends southwards from the high moors. Visible to the west of the road are the remains of an ancient wall running across a moorland shoulder. This is the Deer Dyke, all that is left of a vast enclosed hunting park associated with Kincardine Castle (see p.22). Further on is Fasque. This grand mansion dates

CRATHES CASTLE
A notable venue on Grampian's 'Castle Trail', Crathes Castle is the most popular paying attraction in the north-east.

FASQUE
Still home to the Gladstone family, Fasque was bought in 1829 by John Gladstone. Industrialist and sugar plantation owner, he was also father of W E Gladstone, the four-times Prime Minister.

from 1810 and is owned by the Gladstone family. The house was the home of William Gladstone, Prime Minister in Queen Victoria's time. There is an exhibition of memorabilia relating to this most famous member of the family, otherwise the house is an old-fashioned 'upstairs-downstairs' Victorian stately home. Nearby Fettercairn is a village with a stone arch right in its centre. This was built to commemorate the visit of Queen Victoria and the Prince Consort in 1861. The Fettercairn Distillery offers tours and a chance to sample their single malt, Old Fettercairn.

Between the Grampians and the sea, this part of the old county of Kincardineshire is known as the Mearns (possibly after a supposed brother of King Kenneth II,

Mearnia, said to have acquired this area). The old county name is linked with the old Kincardine Castle near Fettercairn. King Kenneth II was betrayed and murdered here in 995. The castle once guarded the route over the Cairn o' Mount and was a royal hunting seat. Mary, Queen of Scots was just one monarch who stayed there. Very little of it remains as it was demolished in 1646. Even the village of Kincardine has vanished. Overtaken in importance by Stonehaven, its mercat cross was removed to Fettercairn by 1730.

Both the rich red soils of the Howe (hollow) of the Mearns and the rounded heights of the Grampian edge are associated with the Scots writer Lewis Grassic Gibbon (Leslie Mitchell). A visitor centre in the village of Arbuthnott tells the story of this writer, who died at the early age of 34, in 1935. His most famous work was the trilogy *A Scots Quair*. The first part, *Sunset Song*, roots the central character in the Mearns, and uses powerful imagery and distinctive language to build a vivid portrait of farming life with all its tension and toil.

Stonehaven is just one of the many places easily identifiable in the works of Grassic Gibbon. The community here originally grew around the mouths of two small rivers, the Water of Cowie to the north and the Carron to the south. The settlement is associated

with the Keiths, the Earls Marischal of Scotland, who founded the Carron settlement and the harbour. From 1795, new owners, the Quaker Barclays of Urie, laid out a new town between Carron and Cowie. The harbour was improved in time to take part in the expansion of the herring fishery in Victorian times. The story of the town is told in the Tolbooth Museum, in the original seventeenth-century tolbooth built by the Keiths.

The best-preserved Roman earthwork in Grampian lies about 4 miles (6 km) to the north-west.

Raedykes Roman camp dates from AD 83/84 and was a marching camp associated with the northern campaigns of Julius Agricola. He brought the local Picts to battle – the famous Mons Graupius – at a site whose location has never been established. Raedykes has been one suggestion, though Bennachie (see next chapter) is also a contender.

The headquarters of the Earls Marischal was at Dunnottar Castle, south of the town. Essentially a fortified headland, the earliest part of the fortress is its chapel, dating from 1276, and itself built to replace an

STONEHAVEN
Former fishing port, resort and part dormitory town for Aberdeen, Stonehaven is an attractive coastal community.

died during their months of deprivation. (Covenanters were a group who put their signatures to the National Covenant, originally a document opposing King Charles I's church policy.)

A few minutes further down the coast, the Royal Society for the Protection of Birds' reserve at Fowlsheugh is said to be the largest seabird colony in mainland Britain. Some estimates suggest up to 80,000 pairs of six different species breed on the 215 ft (65 m) high cliffs. This includes 30,000 nests each of guillemot and kittiwake, along with smaller numbers of razorbill, fulmar, herring gull and puffin. North of Stonehaven, notably around the spectacular cliffs by Muchalls, is also

ST CYRUS
This national nature reserve is a haven for plants and other wildlife. It consists of a long sandy beach backed by a narrow strip of dunes.

DUNNOTTAR CASTLE *(opposite), became 'Elsinore' for the filming of Franco Zeffirelli's* Hamlet.

early cell established by St Ninian. The tower house dates from the late fourteenth century with the palace complex under way by 1580. Its all but impregnable position enabled it to withstand a siege by Cromwell's army for eight months in 1652.

During this time perhaps the most famous event associated with it took place when the Scottish Regalia (the Crown Jewels) were smuggled out of the castle and hidden in Kinneff Church for the next eight years. In Scotland's troubled religious wars of the seventeenth century Dunnottar also played its gloomy part as the prison for 167 Covenanters who had attended forbidden religious services. Many

puffin country. As burrow nesters, look for them on the softer, grassier portions of the cliff, rather than the sheer rock faces with their tiny ledges favoured by their guillemot and razorbill cousins.

Lovers of wildlife will also enjoy Scottish Natural Heritage's reserve at St Cyrus, to the south on the coast, just within the boundaries of Aberdeenshire where it reaches the sea above Montrose. This, the most southerly of the Grampian beaches, has a grand sweep of sand. Behind it on the old sea cliff, now high above the highest tides, grows a profusion of unusual plants, with several species reaching their most northerly location in Britain.

The River Don is the main river in this central part of Grampian, defining an area called Donside, which parallels Deeside to the south, though it differs from it in landscape character. A very long time ago in geological terms, before glaciers had altered the shape of much of Scotland, the waters from the central Grampian mountains, including the eastern side of the Cairngorms, drained away on a major river system flowing eastwards. To look for the one-time source of the River Don is to find one of Scotland's most remote lochs, Loch Avon, confined within its glacial trough in the heart of the Cairngorms.

Grey screes and granite faces soar upwards from the loch shores to the heights of Cairn Gorm to the north-west, while the loch's outlet runs eastwards through remote Glen Avon. By Inchrory the eastward flow of the River Avon is changed with a sharp bend north. Only a short way further east beyond a low watershed, the River Don is born. The River Avon long ago captured the headwaters of the Don, channelling them off to the River Spey.

Today, the uppermost part of the Don lies in a comparatively little-known stretch of the eastern Grampians. None of the heathery whaleback hills hereabouts reach the magic 3000 ft (914 m) and hence do not attract the attention of walkers who are serious collectors of Scotland's Munros. One burn in particular flows down a hillslope from a spot named the Well of Don about 2200 ft (680 m) high. The little stream, called the Allt an Mhicheil (Michael's Burn), meets with a jumble of headwaters, which gather near what was an old drove road,

running east between Inchrory and Cock Bridge.

By this point, the waters are named the River Don by map makers, and soon after, the infant river has been crossed by its first public road, the famous (or infamous) stretch of the Cock Bridge road on its way to the Lecht ski development and Tomintoul, which always seems to feature first on radio reports of road closures in winter.

It is from this point and downstream that the old rhyme on the Dee and Don valleys rings true: 'The River Dee for fish and tree, the River Don for horn and corn'. From this point the Dee-Don contrasts become apparent, with the underlying rocks the key. The Dee valley has acid granites in its underlying structure, more resistant than the softer sedimentary rocks around the Don, which break down into more fertile soils.

Holding the key to the old routes via Don and Avon, Corgarff Castle has stood in the hollow of the big moors since 1537, when its original oblong tower was built. In 1571, the wife, family and servants of its owner, a Forbes laird, were burned to death during a raid on the castle by the Gordons of Auchindoun. The tragedy is recalled in the old ballad 'Edom o' Gordon'. The castle also played its part in the Jacobite campaigns. Before the ill-fated rising of 1715, the Earl of Mar made his base here. Government troops took over the building after the last uprising in 1746, building the star-shaped curtain wall seen today. Its location on key routes through remote country meant that it was still garrisoned as late as 1831.

By this time, Jacobite plotters were not the target –

CORGARFF CASTLE (opposite). Lost in the rounded heathery hills of upper Donside, Corgarff Castle commanded the road links between Dee, Don and Avon. Its last role was as a garrison for a small troop of soldiers on the lookout for whisky smugglers.

*SNOW NEAR
THE LECHT*
*The Lecht's snowy
reputation owes
much to the A939
Cockbridge to
Tomintoul road,
usually being the
first mentioned on
radio reports when
the weather closes in.*

of Deeside at Crathie (today's B976). The route crosses the River Gairn on a handsome hump-backed bridge now on today's A939. Road travellers on this section, south of the River Don, should look out for mountain hares on the high watershed between Gairn and Dee, as the animals appear to be without any road sense and casualties are frequent. A little further on, a sign to the left points out the old military road where it deviates westwards from today's main road. This old section of road is open to walkers.

The modern road rejoins it by the Cock Bridge, turning north on the steep slopes of the Hill of Allargue to cross the high ground which leads on to the Lecht ski developments, spread out on the rounded, anonymous brown (or white!) hills between Donside and Moray. Snowy winters mean business for upper Donside.

In the other direction, by the village of Strathdon, the now substantial river is flanked by fields of fat cattle, with some sheep on the higher slopes. A sign points to Lonach, a reminder of one of the best-known events in the area. The Lonach Gathering goes back to 1836, part of the wave of interest in Highland matters

instead, the soldiers stationed here had been on the lookout for whisky smuggling which was rife in remote Aberdeenshire at this time. (Further downstream, by Strathdon, Glen Nochty was a notorious route for whisky coming in illicitly to the area from Glenlivet. Any tenants found connected to the trade would lose their tenancy automatically, according to Sir Charles Forbes, local landowner and MP, writing in 1825.)

Corgarff lay on the old military road built by General Caulfeild (Wade's successor). This climbed out which swept Scotland as Gaeldom was seen in an increasingly sentimental light. The Lonach event – essentially Highland Games – is particularly noted for the March of the Lonach Highlanders, who tramp 6 miles in full costume, round all the big houses of the area, pausing for refreshments en route. A horse and cart takes up the rear to pick up stragglers.

Strathdon is also noted for a work barely glimpsed by road travellers. The Doune of Invernochty is a massive mound – a motte or Norman castle earthwork. It is one of the very largest in Scotland, suggesting that the castle that once stood on top of it was an important centre in the network of feudal lordships in what was known as the province of Mar. If danger threatened, the ditch surrounding the motte was flooded using water from a loch close by to the west – a rare example of early military engineering.

To the south of this area lies the 'empty quarter', centred on Morven, where tracks peter out in the brown lands and empty cottar houses are open to the sky. The population has gradually moved to the main glen itself, which retains a strong sense of vitality. In former times there was much movement of cattle over the hill-tracks between Don and Dee.

The Boultenstone Hotel, for example, at the end of Glen Deskry (on the A97) was originally a drovers' inn. The old cattle roads passed around Morven, a hill that is associated with thieves and cattle-reivers. The most famous of these was Patrick Gilroy Macgregor or Gilderoy. He was eventually caught and hanged in Edinburgh in 1658, but not before achieving enough fame to be confused with the better-known Rob Roy MacGregor. This in turn explains the assertion that the

latter used to hide cattle in the Burn o' Vat (see previous chapter on Deeside).

Further on, the ruined Glenbuchat Castle overlooks the Don. This late sixteenth-century Z-plan tower house was originally built by yet another Gordon laird. His direct descendant was 'Old Glenbucket of the 45' – a Jacobite laird whose warlike reputation and fervour for the cause gave King George II nightmares! The story goes that during the 1745 rebellion, 'German Geordie' used to waken in the night screaming 'De great Glenbogget is coming'.

Beyond Glenbuchat, the countryside is gentler and richer, the hills taking a step back. Road and river part company slightly, so that the Don is out of sight of the once-great Kildrummy Castle where it stands on gentle

GLENBUCHAT CASTLE
Sited above the Water of Buchat, this late 16th-century castle needed stout walls and gun-loops for protection, especially when it was owned by ambitious Gordon lairds. John Gordon and Helen Carnegie built it in 1590 – their initials are still visible on a door lintel.

when it was the Earl of Mar's headquarters. It was subsequently dismantled.

The adjacent quarry from where the castle's own stone was won was always part of the fortress's defences. Today, the sheltered hollow is a garden of note; a good range of shrubs and alpines grow here and there is also a water garden.

Downstream, the Don flows on to the Howe of Alford, a pleasantly rural stretch of countryside with hills all around, but set back to give the town of Alford a pleasing and self-contained kind of air. The town has its own Heritage Centre with a large collection of artefacts related mostly to the farming life of the area. There is also a small narrow-gauge railway linking the town to Haughton Country Park. The Grampian Transport Museum is also located here. It specialises in road vehicles and has an extensive collection including vintage snowploughs and the extraordinary 'Craigievar Express'. This was a vertical-boilered three-wheeled contraption that a local postman invented to help him on his round.

The postman must have used this vehicle to deliver letters to Craigievar Castle, which is a few minutes by road south of Alford. This is sometimes described as the most perfect of the Castles of Mar and stands much as the builders left it in 1626. It was built by one William Forbes, also known as 'Danzig Willie' because of his success in the Baltic trade, through which he acquired the wealth for his grand creation. Altogether, the soft pink harling, its wealth of turrets, gables and balustrades have made it the very symbol of Aberdeenshire's wealth of castles. It is in the care of the National Trust for Scotland, who have the difficult task of preventing damage to its structure due to its

STRATHDON COTTAGE
Farming, forestry, tourism and crafts all provide employment for the communities scattered along the valley of the River Don.

KILDRUMMY CASTLE (opposite) was a refuge for King Robert the Bruce's brother during the Scots War of Independence in 1306.

slopes astride the old routes to the fertile lowlands of the north. Kildrummy is a 'castle of enclosure', i.e. built round and enclosing a courtyard. It is one of the very few to survive in Scotland from the thirteenth century, considered to be a high point in medieval castle building in a Europe-wide tradition.

Though initiated by King Alexander II of Scotland, it was while the castle was in the hands of the English King Edward I after 1296 that it was rebuilt, in a style which relates it to castles at Harlech and Caernarvon in Wales, as well as to a number of French examples. The strategic site and strength of Kildrummy ensured its prominent role in the Scots Wars of Independence and beyond. Its last military role was during the 1715 Jacobite uprising,

popularity with visitors.

Back in the Howe of Alford, one of the hills which is prominent – and, in effect, bounds its eastern side – is Bennachie, which is the collective name for a granite 'mini-massif' with distinctive peaks. The River Don skirts the southern edge of this little hill range, perhaps most scenically around the area known as Paradise Wood. The woodlands here were planted after 1713 by Sir Archibald Grant of the Monymusk Estate. He was a famous improver who planted literally millions of trees and recreated much of the 'Forest of Bennachie' which

had for centuries been exploited without thought for the future. The Forestry Commission's Donview Centre, moments from the river, tells the story and is a good centre for walks through the forest and on to high moorland.

Bennachie, as an easterly outlier of the Grampians is a landmark from all directions, thanks mostly to the distinct profile of the Mither Tap (1698 ft, 518 m). A visitor centre on its east side tells the story of the hill and its pattern of settlements. Such a conspicuous landmark has a special place for the local people who

live within sight of its long profile and the 'Baillies of Bennachie' is a conservation society that was formed to protect and conserve the area.

The granite tor of the Mither Tap of Bennachie is flanked by the tumbled stone walls of a fort built around 2000 years ago. Though other prominent points also claim the link, Bennachie is associated with the Battle of Mons Graupius which, according to the Roman historian Tacitus, is where the forces of Agricola, almost at the northern limits of their expedition for that year, finally brought the Caledonian tribes

QUEEN'S VIEW, CROMAR Named after Queen Victoria.

CRAIGIEVAR CASTLE (opposite). Built between the Reformation and later religious wars of the 17th century, Craigievar reflects this peaceful time.

PICARDY STONE   The Pictish symbols include double disc and Z-rod, serpent and mirror.

to battle in AD 83 or 84. The natives were soundly defeated, though the name of their leader Calcagus was recorded as the earliest named inhabitant of Scotland.

The location of Mons Graupius has never been established. Tacitus refers to the place as within sight of the sea in the far north of Scotland. The finding of a Roman marching camp at nearby Durno supports Bennachie's claim but is far from conclusive. The topic is touched on at the unique pre-history park called Archaeolink, at Oyne on the north side of the Bennachie massif. This visitor attraction takes as its theme Grampian's wealth of prehistoric sites, from stone circles of the third millennium BC to Pictish carved stones almost 4000 years younger. As well as models, tableaux, a video presentation and other diversions under cover, there is also a re-creation of an Iron-Age farm and a walk up to an ancient hillfort.

Typical of Grampian's ancient monuments is the Loanhead of Daviot stone circle. North-east Scotland is the heartland of what archaeologists call the recumbent type of stone circle. Usually they are found on or near hilltops with open southerly views and thought to be connected with lunar observations as a kind of calendar for marking seasons – especially important in an early agricultural community. Amid the wealth of speculation surrounding them is the broad agreement that these circles certainly had a ceremonial function and that later they were adapted as burial sites. Loanhead of Daviot is a peaceful spot to pause and speculate on the continuity of settlement and seemingly endless fertility of the north-east soils. All around lie the barley fields and pasture of the agricultural heartlands, still farmed by folk whose preoccupation with the seasons is no

FARMLAND NEAR BENNACHIE   The lands of the Garioch, below the prominent landmark of Bennachie, have been cultivated for thousands of years.

different from that of their far-off ancestors.

Post-dating the recumbent stone circle by at least three millennia (probably more), the Maiden Stone of the ninth century AD is also worth tracking down near Chapel of Garioch on the north-east edge of Bennachie. This is a slab of pink granite. On one side the inscribed cross suggests a late date, probably ninth century, while the other side bears typical Pictish symbols found on other stones in the north-east: an elephant-like Pictish beast, a Z-rod, a mirror and a double-sided comb. Some say these carved stones are some kind of personal memorial, but probably nobody will ever know for certain. The Maiden Stone is one of the very finest to be found in Aberdeenshire.

Back on the River Don (after a tour of Bennachie), Monymusk is also well in sight of the landmark hill. The name of this village is associated with the sacred relic known as the Monymusk Reliquary. This is an eighth-century decorated wooden box that was for long held at the vanished Monymusk Priory. The box contained a bone of St Columba, and was carried before the Scottish army at Bannockburn. Now it is displayed in Edinburgh's Royal Museum of Scotland. The village itself, as seen today, owes much to a late nineteenth-century remodelling by a Grant laird, with Tudor-style cottages and a village green. The village church dates in part from the late twelfth century.

The river flows on past Kemnay, once famed for its silver-grey granite. The main quarry (worked till 1960) was the source of stone used in several bridges on the River Thames. Minutes from the Don and Kemnay to the south is the National Trust for Scotland's property at Castle Fraser. This is the largest of the Castles of Mar, of sophisticated design with a very fine main hall and a walled garden.

The river widens and the pace quickens on the approaches to the town of Inverurie. This busy place once had a locomotive works servicing the stock of the Great North of Scotland Railway. Before that it was the terminus of a short-lived canal (bought over by the new-fangled railway) which ran through to Aberdeen. (The name Port Elphinstone, to the south of the town, survives as a reminder.) Today the town is noted for papermaking and though well within the commuter belt of Aberdeen, has plenty of personality of its own, including a good range of shops.

The Don winds on eastward through broad river flats, grazed by overwintering grey geese, on its way to Kintore, Dyce and the sea. The main road north and west leaves the Don valley in the opposite direction, following the valley of the River Urie, tributary of the Don, upstream. The road, ultimately to Inverness, passes through the Garioch (pronounced 'Geerie'). Like Buchan out in the north-east corner, this was formerly one of the area's ancient lordships. Its fertility attracted early settlements and, in consequence, a rich heritage of prehistoric remains, such as the Loanhead Stone Circle and many others. The name of the area is also recalled in the local malt whisky, Glen Garioch, distilled in Oldmeldrum.

The Aberdeen-Inverness road leaves the Garioch by the Glens of Foudland. High on the hills above the road, tracks and stone heaps can still be made out among the heather. This is all that is left of the Foudland slate quarries. The roofing slate formerly worked here still gives many older buildings in

CASTLE FRASER (opposite). This fine castle started life as a simple rectangular keep dating from the mid 15th century. Another square tower and, diagonally opposite, a round tower, were added a century later. Further works were completed before 1636 and subsequent 19th-century additions created the complex structure of today.

Aberdeenshire – most famously Balmoral Castle – their characteristic bluish colour. The quarries reached their peak output in the 1850s, with 800,000–900,000 slates produced annually.

Beyond the Garioch to the west (but visible from it) is the distinct crouching profile of the Tap o' Noth. At 1847 ft (563 m) its curious flattened summit is the second highest hillfort in Scotland, contained within a wall running all round the hilltop. Its first phase of occupation is dated early first millennium BC, on the strength of the outlines of platforms high on the hill which have been interpreted as hut sites. Habitation this high today is cold and inhospitable and suggests that the place was occupied before the climate deteriorated in the first millennium BC.

The Tap o' Noth rises out of a bright green sea, with a high tide mark of yellow gorse all around it in spring. The prevailing greenness is a reminder that this is the edge of the Grampians, and the boulder clays dumped by glaciers have been worked over by generations of farmers to create some of the finest of Scotland's agricultural land. Close to the Tap o' Noth, these green seas surround places like Lumsden – rather unexpectedly, the home of the Scottish Sculpture Workshop – or Rhynie, immediately below the Tap o' Noth. Likewise half lost in the wide fields in this wide bowl below the hills is the little village of Clatt, whose name comes from the Gaelic 'cleith' meaning concealed, a fitting description for this quiet spot (though its village hall comes alive at weekends with tea and home baking!). There is a particularly fine prospect of this end of Grampian, overlooked by the Tap o' Noth, from Suie Hill, south of Clatt.

Rhynie and Lumsden lie on an old route coming north from the Dee and Don via Kildrummy. This route meets the main Aberdeen to Inverness road at the town of Huntly which sits at the centre of an area called Strathbogie, from the River Bogie flowing north to join the Deveron. The older part of the town as seen today was laid out in the eighteenth century by the Duke of Gordon and is associated with a senior branch of the Gordons, whose former power-base was at Huntly Castle. Huntly has its own self-contained air, with shops of modest scale on the streets leading away from the handsome main square. It still has a role as a community that depends on the prosperous agricultural hinterland round about it.

Huntly Castle is today a handsome ruin, sitting on top of a twelfth-century motte overlooking the River Deveron. The original work was replaced by an L-plan tower in the early fifteenth century, then rebuilt later in the same century, further remodelled a century later, then adorned with heraldic work in the early seventeenth century. The 'Gey Gordons' led the opposition to the Reformation but their power was curbed by Mary, Queen of Scots, at the Battle of Corrichie (fought near Banchory) in 1562. Afterwards, Huntly Castle was sacked. The Gordons also fared badly in the religious wars of the seventeenth century, with the second Marquis of Huntly beheaded in 1649, and thereafter his grand castle falling into decay.

Going north beyond Huntly, essentially inland and rural, there are the first hints of a cooler air, and the faintest taste of salt on the north wind. The sea is in sight after a drive of about 20 minutes and farming gives way to fishing.

HUNTLY CASTLE (opposite). The third castle to be built to guard the crossing of the River Deveron, the ruins of this once-grand palace are a memorial to the former power of the Gordons. The frieze of large letters adorning the building commemorates George Gordon, First Marquis of Huntly.

The Roads to Buchan

Robert Burns on his Highland tour, Doctor Johnson, the English lexicographer, with James Boswell hanging on his every word, even Thomas Pennant, one of the earliest travel writers – all of these travellers toured in Grampian in the eighteenth century. They all, to a greater or lesser extent, 'cut off the corner'. This is in keeping with a kind of perception that still exists today of the 'far' north-east – the tip of Buchan: that it is really a very long way off and that there is not very much to see. Small wonder that the folk of Buchan are self-reliant and self-contained, though friendly. With Aberdeen the main city to the south, these farming and fishing folk have a different perception of Scotland, and a sometimes acute awareness that the priorities of the central belt of Scotland, its politics and its media, do not always coincide with this other northern Scotland.

In general, the landscapes of Buchan and its approaches are essentially man-made, recording the generations of toil of the farmers who turned the mosses and heathy scrub of this northern edge into fertile fields. In a few places, corners of these mosses remain in their unclaimed form, as a reminder of the look of the land before the age of the improvers from the eighteenth century onwards. Similarly, as the nineteenth century progressed, fishing became increasingly important, at first from small ports and in places without harbours, even from open beachs; latterly from larger harbours to match the demands and the increasing size of the catching vessels.

With a coastline running for more than 100 miles (160 km), this leaves the essential landscape of north-east Scotland as one of cultivation – almost, but not quite, to the cliff or beach, with only steep-sided coastal valleys (often ancient glacier meltwater channels) uncultivated. These 'dens', as they are known in Buchan, with their stunted woodland or deep bracken, are important wildlife havens, often providing cover for roe deer or badgers, creatures more associated with inland woods elsewhere.

In fact, much of the natural habitat of the coastline is steep-sided, if not vertical. Field gives way to fence, then a narrow strip of coastal heath or woodrush, followed by a precipitous face, often hung with wildflowers, on a rockface that tumbles to an unspoilt shoreline. Away from the sandy beaches, this is the typical coastal profile of the north-east. In short, the special coastline is one of the most attractive features of the north-east corner.

It starts with the endless sweep of sand north from the estuary of the River Don. For ten unbroken miles (16 km) the sand stretches practically out of sight into a haze of sea-spray until it meets with the estuary of the River Ythan at the Sands of Forvie. So straight and easy runs the coastline here that the dunes inland were the site of the 5-mile-(8-km)-long base line used as a starting point for all other measurements by triangulation for the first (1817) Ordnance Survey in Scotland.

The River Ythan (pronounced '*eye*-than'), strictly speaking, flows through Formartine (pronounced 'for-*mar*-tin'), rather than Buchan. The dune complex on the northern edge of the Ythan estuary has been a national nature reserve since 1959, known as the Sands of Forvie. A nearby field station is used by Aberdeen University and the complex ecology of estuary and

SANDS OF FORVIE (opposite). With its wind-blown sand dune system and coastal heath, the national nature reserve at Sands of Forvie is an important centre for wildlife. The reserve is noted for its unspoiled beauty and is a sanctuary for the highest concentration of breeding eider ducks in Britain. Flint arrow heads among the sand, prehistoric 'shell-middens' (shell-heaps), Bronze and Iron-Age hut circles, cairns and stone clearance heaps all point to a series of ancient settlements which once thrived here too.

Perhaps the most famous visitor to the former fishing village of Collieston was T E Lawrence (Lawrence of Arabia), on leave from the RAF and hiding away from the world. He wrote of the 'sand-tussocked desolation', and spent his time walking and feeding the gulls. All around lies a smugglers' coast and there is even a cave called the Gin Hole, recalling just one of the contraband products brought ashore by the 'free traders' of the late eighteenth and early nineteenth centuries.

Further north, the clifftop community of Whinnyfold is the very essence of the bracing

CRUDEN BAY
The former Great North of Scotland Railway attempted to develop Cruden Bay as a golfing resort. Today, the railway and its hotel are gone, but the golf course remains as one of Scotland's finest links.

dune has been extensively studied. A visitor centre run by Scottish Natural Heritage has been set up by Collieston to the north. 'Migrating' dunes, fixed dunes, grey mature dunes, coastal heath and cliff are all to be found in a comparatively small area, along with Britain's highest concentration of breeding eider duck. In places on the reserve, the 'aa-ha' calls of these sea-going ducks intersperse – perhaps uniquely – with the croaking of red grouse; birds usually associated with upland moors.

bleakness of this stretch of coast. Why a group of fishers would choose to use the treacherous, rock-toothed bay below can scarcely be credited, but as late as 1929, there were still 19 fishers recorded living here. (However, there is a suspicion that some of these coastal spots were settled because of the smuggling trade rather than fishing!) Some Whinnyfold fishers migrated a little way northward to Cruden Bay, or, more accurately, Port Erroll, the fishing village recalling the name of its founder, the local landowner, the Earl of Erroll. This is a most attractive spot, tucked out of the north wind and facing the peerless crescent of orange sand backed by one of the most famous golf courses in the north.

The grim and roofless outline of Slains Castle, the former home of the Earls of Erroll, is visible from the Cruden Bay road approaches. Johnson and Boswell enjoyed hospitality here in 1773 and in recent years the association of the place as an inspiration for Bram Stoker's *Dracula* has been heavily promoted. Though it sounds unlikely, Stoker holidayed at Whinnyfold and, it is said, retired there.

Equally sinister, however, is the atmosphere around the Bullers of Buchan. This place is hard to describe it is a kind of great sea hole in the cliff, in which the unsettling voices of kittiwakes wail and echo. Johnson and Boswell were taken in by boat and Johnson, ever mindful of his role as a dictionary editor, remarked how the rock seemed 'perpendicularly tubulated'. Yet another former fishing settlement stands close by, though most fishers had gone to Peterhead by the beginning of the twentieth century.

A little way north, Peterhead offers a safe haven for vessels sailing on this granite-toothed coast. The quarries to the south of the town (near the village confusingly named Stirling) were the source of the red granite which gives the town its characteristic colour. The first modern harbour was built here from 1773, while the harbour of refuge that extends its arms around the bay was built from 1889 using convict labour from the newly opened Peterhead Prison. In the 1820s the town was the largest whaling port in Britain. A herring boom followed on. Today, the town

is still busy thanks to its role as Europe's largest white fish landing port. It also has a food-processing plant and services the offshore oil activities.

Hard to believe today in this single-minded town, but Peterhead's main attempt to diversify away from the produce of the sea came about before the end of the eighteenth century when it became noted as a spa resort. However, building work around the harbour area, where the main well and sea-bathing facilities were at the time, may have resulted in a deterioration in the local waters' quality and the demise of the town as a fashionable resort.

North of Peterhead, more golden sands roll out, past the St Fergus gas terminal, past Rattray Head lighthouse on its offshore plinth, and on to separate the

SLAINS CASTLE Begun by the ninth Earl of Errol in 1597, Slains started as a tower, was expanded into a quadrangle of buildings and later remodelled in 1836. The changing fortunes of the later Earls meant it was abandoned in 1925.

KINNAIRD HEAD LIGHTHOUSE
Visitors can enjoy breathtaking views from here as part of their visit to the Museum of Scottish Lighthouses.

Loch of Strathbeg from the sea. Strathbeg is Scotland's largest land-locked coastal lagoon and a wintering post for wildfowl of international importance. At peak time its bird population amounts to 35,000 including large numbers of pink-footed and greylag geese. Close views can be obtained from the Royal Society for the Protection of Birds' visitor centre at Starnafin Farm which is on the west side of the loch. (Approach from the village of Crimond.)

The Rattray and Strathbeg area have their own special atmosphere, with hoary lichen-encrusted ancient dunes and a sense of desolation and remoteness. Small wonder that a former fishing settlement here, founded in the last quarter of the eighteenth century, was soon called Botany Bay,

comparing it to the Australian penal colony established in 1788. All that remains of Botany, the sea-town of Rattrayhead today, is a line of ruined cottages at the south end of the loch.

More sands run past the villages of St Combs and Cairnbulg, places described by the north-east writer Cuthbert Graham as built 'in one of the most ruthlessly exposed places of human habitation in Britain'. Sandy shores lead on round the pleasing curve of Fraserburgh Bay to the town of Fraserburgh. Here 'King Herring' once ruled supreme, providing the money for the grand Victorian houses which line some of the older streets in the town. From 1857 onwards, imaginative harbour works including an 1875-1883 breakwater expansion which was one of the first seaworks to use concrete extensively, transformed the modest port into the leading herring port in Scotland before the twentieth century began. Today, like its rival, Peterhead, Fraserburgh is still dependent on fishing, a story recalled in the town's heritage centre.

Fraserburgh is also the home of the Museum of Scottish Lighthouses, adjacent to the earliest light built by the Northern Lighthouse Commissioners in 1787. This is Kinnaird Head, the turning point for the Moray Firth. A visit to the museum here includes both a close look at the display of lighthouse paraphernalia, reflectors, lenses, models and so on, and a guided tour of the lighthouse itself. The light is constructed through and on top of a sixteenth-century castle built by Sir Alexander Fraser. Sir Walter Scott himself (who came here on board the *Pharos*, the Commissioners' own lighthouse inspection vessel) had a hand in preserving this unique castle conversion.

Westward, the sands give way to rocky shores, a point that can be noted from the top of the lighthouse tower. Past little settlements once bound up with the sea such as Sandhaven and Rosehearty, the coast begins to rise in great cliffs. A little road leads down to the caves in the red sandstone of Aberdour beach. Cliffs rise again westwards, the ramparts breached by the road that leads down to Pennan. This is the first of three especially attractive villages on this overlooked coastline.

Pennan sits gable-end to the shore. Sea and houses are separated by little more than the width of a roadway. In time of storms, the locals fit shutters on to their most vulnerable windows lest the waves fling up stones. The village's profile

was raised in 1983 with the release of the gently quirky and environmentally friendly film *Local Hero*. The village's phonebox was given a starring role as the means by which Macintyre (Peter Riegert), the executive who eventually falls in love with the place, communicates with his boss across the Atlantic, Happer (Burt Lancaster). Today, visitors still come to be photographed beside the red kiosk, though in the film it was resited on the pier to make it more photogenic!

West of the village, the coast road runs past a signpost to Cullykhan, where there is a carpark; this headland was fortified first in the Iron Age and most

recently in the Napoleonic Wars. Just beyond it is the curious gash known as Hell's Lum, from the way the sea-spray smokes out of this subterranean cliff gallery during storms. Westwards again, the cliffs rise past scattered seabird colonies to their highest point at Troup Head. Nearby, slippery grass and a crumbling cliff edge make the view of Scotland's only mainland gannet colony a hazardous expedition, only accessible to well-shod walkers and entirely unsuitable for young children. The main colonies of auks (including puffins) and kittiwakes can be viewed slightly more safely from just west of the headland.

PENNAN
Originally a fishing settlement, today Pennan has its share of holiday homes, but also has a permanent all-year-round community. The village is reached by a steep and twisting road.

The villages of Crovie and Gardenstown lie further round this cliff-girt coast. Describing Gardenstown, the Revd John Pratt, in his famous work, *Buchan*, (1858), relates how 'we descend from terrace to terrace, and look down into the very chimneys of the houses below. The situation is singularly striking. The houses are perfect eyries, built on ledges, and in the recesses of the cliff.' Though the access road of today is less demanding than in Pratt's time, the old part of Gardenstown (or Gamrie as the locals call it, from the parish name) is one of the most spectacularly sited villages anywhere in Scotland.

However, its neighbour Crovie can also claim a special location. If Pennan is close to the sea, then Crovie is practically in it, as high tides with strong winds have more than once punched holes in the concrete plinth which holds the gable-ends of these houses above the water line. So narrow is the space between house wall and shore that there is no vehicular access and every stick of household furniture in the village was, at one time or another, carried in by hand. Crovie is essentially a holiday village. The fishermen who formerly lived here sold out after the worst storm in living memory, in January 1953. They mostly moved to the upper, newer part of Gardenstown, which is linked to Crovie by a coastal path (likewise washed away and replaced since 1953!)

The layout of Gamrie and its neighbour can best be seen from the ruined Kirk of St John the Evangelist, on the heady slopes of Gamrie Mor, the headland west of the village. This kirk is associated with the successful defeat of a party of raiding Danes, remnant of a force already defeated at a battle at Aberlemno in Angus. The Norsemen arrived by sea but the local Pictish mormaor (chieftain) was able to muster enough men at arms to beat off the attack and consequently founded the kirk in thanksgiving. From here to Macduff is a further stretch of wild coast, seldom tramped and all but pathless.

Macduff is another little grey fishing town, noted for its traditional boat-building skills. Its name recalls the noted 'improver' James Duff, Earl of Fife, who re-designed the old fishing settlement of Doune. The town became a Burgh of Barony in 1783. Today, the Macduff Marine Aquarium draws visitors to the town. They come to admire the growing kelp reef in the aquarium's centrepiece: an 88,000 gallon (400,000 litre) tank, 32 ft (10 m) across. Unique among British aquaria, this open-topped tank allows natural daylight to penetrate the water, creating conditions for a range of marine plants to grow, which provide a diverse habitat for a thriving colony of local fish and invertebrates.

Macduff's neighbour is Banff, facing it across the mouth of the River Deveron, spanned by a handsome seven-arched bridge designed by John Smeaton (1779). Banff is the older of the two settlements, having a burgh charter granted in 1324 by King Robert I. As long ago as the twelfth century it was one of the trading ports in the 'Northern Hanse' – a group of burghs with European trading links. Its prosperity eventually allowed expansion away from its little harbour and up the shelved hill beyond, where today's High Street runs. Banff's architectural heritage is outstanding and includes examples of domestic architecture from the sixteenth century onwards.

Perhaps unexpectedly, Banff is also the setting for

CROVIE (opposite). Mostly, but not entirely, a cluster of holiday homes today, Crovie has the narrowest space between shore and cliff of any Scottish village. Among many tales of high tides and gales on this coast, memories of the 1953 storm are still strong. It caused much damage and is said to have been the highest tide ever recorded.

DUFF HOUSE
William Adam
the architect could
certainly size up
a client. He created a
building since described
as 'swaggering,
vainglorious and
intimidating' – to
suit the ambitious
Lord Braco.

the principal outstation of the National Galleries of Scotland. Duff House was constructed from 1735 onwards by the noted Scottish architect William Adam for Lord Braco, Earl of Fife. After a dispute with the architect, the house was never actually occupied by its owner. The house was gifted to the town when the estates were sold off in 1906. It opened in its present role, as a country-house gallery, in 1995.

Continuing westward, Whitehills sets the scene for a distinctive group of Moray Firth communities, with its neatly painted (former) fishers' houses and a harbour not yet entirely given over to pleasure craft. The little town is also typical of the north-east in that local fish-processing businesses sell the finest seafood at reasonable prices. The same applies to the next village, Portsoy. This is an even more scenic place, its harbour area with its eighteenth-century warehousing and merchants' houses, many restored, recalling its heyday as an important Firth port. The harbour is thought to be the earliest on the Moray Firth, dating from 1692. The period feel to the harbourfront has been exploited in the past by film and TV companies looking for authentic settings.

There is a pleasant coastal walk to the sandy beach that gave the little coastal village of Sandend its name. Here again, there is character in plenty down by its small harbour.

There has been fishing from this village since at least 1624, the date recorded in the local kirk's minutes when the villagers were rebuked by the Kirk Session for baiting lines on Sunday! The harbour in its present form dates from 1883. Walkers can also leave the village westwards by the rocky shore. This path leads on to Findlater Castle, founded by the Ogilvies and strengthened on the orders of King James II in 1455. Little remains today except the vaults of this spectacularly sited fortress perched on its rocky headland. This draughty place was abandoned when the Ogilvies completed the much grander Cullen House at Cullen.

A walk to Findlater Castle is possible from a farm-yard carpark (signposted). From here the path also leads on to Sunnyside Beach, arguably one of the very finest of the Moray Firth beaches (particularly as it requires a little effort to get there). Beyond, is the border with Moray, and the little coastal gem of Cullen.

Inland Buchan lacks the grandeur of the western half of Grampian. Landmark hills like Bennachie, Ben Rinnes or the Tap o' Noth are glimpsed from time to time on the rural road network. All around are gentle slopes, for though the area is known as the Buchan Plain, it is far from level; it is a series of gentle cultivated slopes. Towns, in the main, are small. The main one is Turriff, for centuries a market-centre in the middle of this well-cultivated landscape.

Turriff's origins go back as far as the seat of a Pictish ruler, Lathmon, probably predating the ruins of the town's eleventh-century Auld Kirk, as seen today, by about 500 years. The site here is associated with Pictish missionary St Congan. After the age of improvement dawned and local farms were enclosed, Turriff was the centre point for many a farmworker's life, as it was an important 'feein market' or hiring fair. These markets were held twice a year and agricultural workers of all types could contract themselves for a six-month term to the local farmers. Turriff's agricultural life is now focussed on the 'Turra Show', an annual event, and the largest agricultural show of its kind in the north of Scotland.

To set the rural life of Buchan in context, visit Aden County Park. Here in the former estate of Aden, one of the area's grand houses stands as a roofless shell (perhaps a salutary warning for other estate owners).

The estate's home farm steading is now the setting for the Aberdeenshire Farming Museum. This tells the story of the land in an exhibition themed as 'The Weel Vrought Grun' (the well-worked ground). There is also a re-creation of a working farm of the 1950s.

The great improving landlords of the eighteenth and nineteenth centuries did not restrict their efforts to agriculture but attempted to introduce new industries to Buchan. These, they saw taking place in their planned villages — usually recognisable because of their regular or grid-iron plan. Strichen, founded in 1764 by Lord Strichen, is typical, with its houses opening directly on to the street but with large back gardens. (Contemporary thinking was that if houses had no grounds at the front, their inhabitants would

FINDLATER DOOCOT
This is an early dovecot (Scots: doocot), dating from the 16th century. The pigeons were used as a food source by the local estate.

FYVIE CASTLE
Passing through the hands of Prestons, Meldrums, Setons, Gordons and Forbes-Leiths, a 13th-century defensive quadrangle became a grand baronial castle over the centuries.

be less inclined to turn them into dung heaps and hence make the place look untidy!) New Pitsligo (William Forbes, 1787) is another example. Forbes actively promoted his settlement, with textiles and lace-making originally the mainstay.

Similarly, Cuminestown recalls the linen manufacturer Sir Joseph Cumine, while Lumsden, New Byth, Longside and many other places have parallel stories to tell. Perhaps most revealingly, Lord Strichen named another of his little settlements New Leeds, suggesting his ambitions for this project, which was intended to make its mark on the textile industry.

However, not all Buchan's villages fall into this improved category. Others grew up as the religious centres for their local parish and have a less ordered shape. The most picturesque of these 'kirk-touns' is Fordyce, a little way inland from Sandend. For many years it held a fair and market within the kirkyard of its ancient church – a tradition which may have led to the local minister commenting in the *Statistical Account 1791-1799* that he still had to 'make a step through the village, after dinner, and break up drinking parties.' Unfortunately, Fordyce has no ale-house today but is much visited for its higgledy-piggledy quaintness –

perhaps a little unexpected in the barleyfields of Banffshire.

Finally, though the main concentration of castles lies in the southern half of Grampian, there are some architectural treasures to discover. At Fyvie Castle a medieval castle of enclosure (i.e. built round a court-yard) was transformed over the centuries into a grand baronial masterpiece, a rambling part-fortress, part stately home now in the care of the National Trust for Scotland (NTS). By contrast, and altogether lighter, is Haddo House, built to the design of William Adam from 1731 onwards and surrounded by its 'policies' (estate grounds) which also function as a county park. As at Fyvie, the NTS also have a presence at Haddo.

As for gardens in the spare landscape of the north-east, the plantspeople of this corner are ever optimistic, though salt-laden coastal gales play havoc with coastal gardens. Both fishermen and farmers are traditionally apathetic about lush shows of vegetation (and in former days had no time for such frivolities anyway!) However, the north-east traveller in search of interesting gardens can find some surprises, mostly in the form of private houses which open them under Scotland's Gardens Scheme. Perhaps the most unexpected show is at Pitmedden Gardens, a re-creation of a seventeenth-century garden, originally built by Sir Alexander Seton. The NTS look after 40,000 bedding plants and 3 miles of box hedges in complex patterns – quite unusual on the edge of bleak Buchan.

With just a few exceptions, the land of the north-east corner is certainly austere in many places. Yet the old county of Banffshire is a kind of bridge between bare Buchan and the comparative lushness of Moray which lies to the west.

PITMEDDEN GARDENS
Alexander Seton, Lord Pitmedden, retired as a Law Lord to pursue his life's work: creating a formal or 'great' garden. A date stone records its founding as 2 May 1675.

Moray

Moray today has a separate administration from Aberdeenshire. It is an area full of distinctive features, from a landscape point of view, especially the simple fact that its high ground lies in the south. This in turn creates the very pleasing set of weather statistics of which Moray boasts, basically comprising exceptional sunshine hours and low rainfall figures (in Scottish terms). For example, Forres has more sunshine than Edinburgh, while Lossiemouth has about the same rainfall as London. All of this is due to the 'rain shadow' effect of the Grampians to the south which catch the rain and cloud from the prevailing south-wester-lies, allowing a dry, warmer wind to blow down to the well-favoured ground to the north. (This is really the 'föhn effect', so-called from the name given to the wind off the lee side of the Alps.)

The part of Moray which benefits most is a fertile low-lying stretch between moor and coast known as the Laich of Moray, originally from a Norse word *lagr* meaning low. This plain runs from the River Spey west to Forres, a distance of around 30 miles (48 km). In former times much of it was marshy, notably between Elgin and Lossiemouth. The motte of Duffus Castle, with its huge curtain walls, must once have risen like an island out of the marshy wastes. Duffus is sometimes described as the finest of the north's Norman motte-and-bailey castles; it dates from around 1300 and was the former seat of the de Moravia family. Drainage and reclamation over the centuries created the green and wooded scene of today. The light rains and mild climate make conditions right for growing barley, the very best going as malting for the area's thriving whisky-distilling industry.

Moray's coastline is as attractive as the easterly part of the Moray Firth, with similar tales to tell of fishing settlements on a rugged coast, though there are also some superb sands. River estuaries diversify the habitat and have their own special wildlife features. For example, in other parts of Scotland, ospreys are rare creatures. On the Spey they flourish and on the stretch between Fochabers and the sea, they are common enough to barely excite comment. They can be seen from the windows of Baxters of Speyside's restaurant, or without even leaving the car, at Spey Bay, by the Tugnet Ice House.

The River Lossie is closely confined by woodland almost to its estuary. The pines here, within sound of the sea, are the haunt of crested tits, those denizens of pinewoods, usually associated with upper Speyside. All of the river mouths, from Spey to Findhorn and beyond, are also good places to look for the Moray Firth's resident bottlenose dolphins. Here in the Firth they grow larger than anywhere else in the world, the cold but nutrient-rich waters providing them with the food for laying down a thick layer of blubber.

Upland Moray can be explored by means of the Spey and its tributaries, alongside which run the main lines of communication (though, sadly, no longer a railway). The Speyside Way, a designated long-distance footpath, allows a closer exploration. From Tugnet at the mouth of the Spey to Tomintoul, it allows at least 48 miles (79 km) of walking. At Craigellachie, the path takes to the trackbed of the now-abandoned Great North of Scotland Railway. Beyond Aberlour, the walking route goes past distilleries at Carron,

RIVER AVON NEAR TOMINTOUL (opposite). The River Avon is flowing north at this point, on its way to confluence with the Spey. This part of the glen, particularly around Delnabo, was once the place of refuge for a branch of the Clan Gregor, more usually associated with the Trossachs. The clan was proscribed in the 17th century and the chief of the Glenstrae sept married into a local family of Grants.

**GLEN AVON
IN SNOW**
*Upland Moray, near
Tomintoul, with its
open moors and plan-
tations, has its own
special atmosphere.*

Knockando and Tamdhu and it can be appreciated how the whisky industry fits in to the landscape. Nowhere in this part of Moray is far from the sight of a gentle plume of steam floating above the trees as the business continues endlessly of converting pure water, barley and yeast into a pleasurable product.

Many place-names in Moray have given their names to malt whiskies, or more accurately, single malts. A single malt whisky is the product of one distillery only, using only malted barley. No blending of other grain whiskies is involved. Each malt whisky has its own characteristic nose and taste, attributed to the shape of the copper still, the water supply, the degree of peatiness imparted by the smoke from the fire which dries the grain, the skill of the craftsmen, and other less definable qualities.

The special character of the Speyside malts seems to be a lightness and sweetness, and there are plenty of opportunities to test this out by following signs on the unique Malt Whisky Trail, which allows much comparing and contrasting of malt whiskies at a number of distilleries, all of which do tours and tastings – an essential part of the experience of Moray.

Further on, the route leaves the gentle gradients of the trackbed for the Braes of Glenlivet en route for Tomintoul. Upland Moray with its open moors and plantations has its own special atmosphere – not quite into the very highest hills, yet attractively remote and self-contained.

The high ground rising to the south naturally shapes the story of Moray in the same way as it does eastwards in the far corner of Grampian. The 'Grampian cocoon' effect, historically speaking, applies to Moray as well, as a place that has sometimes lain apart from the mainstream of Scottish affairs. Yet, in a historical context, it seems that Moray's position north of the Grampian mountains has always given it autonomy, real or imagined, and that the allegiances or affiliations of its rulers were quite important in Scottish politics from the Middle Ages onwards.

With autonomy in mind it is not surprising to note that the very centre of ancient Pictland in the Dark Ages has been suggested as lying around the promontory of Burghead on the shores of the Moray Firth. There is a case for arguing that the Battle of Mons Graupius, when Roman expeditionary forces challenged the Pictish rule in the northland, was not around Bennachie (see previous chapter) but further north around the River Isla in the vicinity of Keith, with two far northern marching camps at Auchinhove and Muiryfold as evidence.

After Picts and Scots were united and Viking threats overcome, the aftershocks of the Norman conquest and the introduction of the feudal system arrived late in Moray, with the old-style Celtic thanes and mormaors hanging on until the old House of Moray was overthrown in 1130 during the reign of King David I. The line which became the new-style Earls of Moray came in their place.

Gradually, the full flourishing of the feudal system in these northlands took place. As in other parts of the country, the lords held their landholdings or baronies round their castles. Places of strategic importance evolved into royal castles, often with a royal burgh nearby. The bishop of the Diocese of Moray was the most powerful religious figure in the area. His fortified residence at Spynie Palace is a reminder of medieval times in Moray, as are the much altered fortresses such as Lochindorb, Duffus and Darnaway Castles. As for the burghs themselves, towns like Elgin and Forres still thrive. Even the street plans at the core of these two towns are a reminder that they go back a long way.

During the Scottish Wars of Independence of the thirteenth and fourteenth centuries, Moray was the most northerly territory occupied by King

Edward of England's forces in 1296. In the next year, Andrew de Moravia ('of Moray') was appointed Guardian of Scotland and fought with William Wallace at Stirling Bridge. Later, the Bishop of Moray, David de Moravia, was a firm supporter of King Robert I in the Bannockburn campaign and the final victory.

In the later Middle Ages, Moray provided a good example of the kind of instability that was to disturb Scotland repeatedly through the centuries. Among the squabbling offspring of the timid King Robert II was his fourth son, Alexander Stewart, who had landholdings in the Badenoch and Strathspey area, and held his

BEN RINNES from Craigellachie. Though small in comparison with its high Cairngorm neighbours to the south-west, the distinctive gentle cone of Ben Rinnes is a landmark from many points to the east and north.

father's authority in the north. This brought him into conflict with the Bishop of Moray. The clash of crown and church grew to the extent that on hearing of criticism by the bishop, Alexander razed the town of Forres in retaliation in 1390, following up the dramatic deed by burning down Elgin Cathedral. His powerbase was at Lochindorb, an island fortress out in the featureless moors north of Grantown-on-Spey. For his reign of terror in Moray, he subsequently acquired the name of 'The Wolf of Badenoch', and was excommunicated. Though linked by birth with the House of Stewart and Scotland's ruling family, he used the uplands in the south of Moray as a haven for his predations on the gentler lowland to the north.

Another threat to the peace of the province occurred when the powerful Earldom of Moray, in the murky politics of the day, was acquired by the mighty Douglas family in the mid fifteenth century. They too mounted their challenge to the authority of the crown and were only with difficulty defeated by King James II in 1455. Not until after the Reformation was Moray left in comparative peace. Eventually, Bishop Lesley was to describe his lands as 'by all the rest commendet with us for baith plentie and pleisure'. By 1727, even with the Jacobite question unresolved, Moray was in an expansionist mood. Lossiemouth had been founded as a new port for Elgin about two decades before. Daniel Defoe was politically active as a government spy, as well as a writer, when he reported, on passing through the area, that Moray was 'a pleasant country, the soil fruitful, watered with fine rivers, and full of good towns.'

By the end of the eighteenth century, the Age of Improvement was bringing new planned towns to the area (which is why so many of Moray's little towns are built to the familiar grid pattern). Next came the railways, with the now-vanished Lossiemouth to Elgin connection opened as early as 1852, the very first in the north of Scotland. Later, Cullen and Lossiemouth, with their rail connections, flourished in the new enthusiasm for bracing seaside holidays. With modern tourism based more on activity holidays, traditional seaside resorts are less of a magnet, in common with other parts of Scotland – but the Speyside Way, the wealth of golf courses, and the signposted Whisky Trail all have their contribution to make to Moray's economy.

The administrative centre of Moray is Elgin, the second-largest place in the north-east, after Aberdeen. Known as 'The Lantern of the North', Elgin Cathedral was founded in 1224 as the seat of the Diocese of Moray. Barely surviving its attack by the Wolf of Badenoch, the cathedral was rebuilt and continued in use until the Reformation. In common with so many other grand religious buildings in Scotland, it fell into disrepair as a consequence. Its central tower collapsed in 1711 and stonework was gradually carried away for use in other parts of the town. However, as early as 1825, plans were made to take the ruin into care.

Today, it is still possible to climb high into the cathedral's west towers (where there is a fine view down to a recently created 'Biblical Garden' adjacent) and view the overall setting on the low grounds by the winding river, with the rooftops of the town below and a low ridge westwards. On this ridge perches the tiniest fragment of old Elgin Castle, over-shadowed by the Doric column which is the 1839 monument to the Duke of Gordon.

ELGIN CATHEDRAL (opposite). Some have described Elgin Cathedral as Scotland's most beautiful cathedral. Its exceptionally wide nave is unique in Scotland, while the chapter house is the finest of its kind. After the Reformation, the lead was off the cathedral roof by 1567, its rood screen gone by 1640 while the central tower collapsed in 1711.

SPYNIE PALACE represents the power of the church in medieval times. The site consists of a 14th-century courtyard castle and the massive 15th-century Davy's Tower (after Bishop David Stewart).

Away from the cathedral, Elgin's High Street is dominated by St Giles Kirk, built in 1827-8 on the site of the original parish church. On either side narrow lanes run off like fish-bones from a central spine, echoing the original layout of the town. Some eighteenth-century work survives at the east end of the High Street in the form of arcaded shop fronts, once a noted feature of the town. Elgin today has a busy commercial centre, drawing its trade from all sides (though less so from the west with the continuing growth of Inverness). The nearby RAF bases at Lossiemouth and Kinloss are important in the local economy. Elgin is also noted as the setting for the Cashmere Visitor Centre (Johnston's of Elgin), manufacturing high-quality knitwear for the very top

end of the market. Nearby, Elgin Museum tells the story of the town and features among its wide-ranging collection fossils found locally that represent some of Britain's earliest dinosaurs.

On the road north to Lossiemouth, the ruins of Spynie Palace are in the care of Historic Scotland. The nearby old kirkyard of Spynie is the last resting place of James Ramsay MacDonald, first Labour Prime Minister. He was born at Lossiemouth, a connection explored by the town's museum. Clear conditions and low rainfall are factors which in turn helped Lossiemouth establish itself as a golfing resort and then as a busy RAF airbase. Lossiemouth was also a noted fishing port. The first 'Zulu' type fishing boat was designed and built by a local fisherman in 1879. (Its name recalls the Zulu Wars which were being fought at the time.) Arguably, the port also has a claim for the first design of a modern seine net vessel, though today Lossiemouth comes some way behind major ports such as Peterhead and Fraserburgh.

Going west beyond Covesea Skerries Lighthouse, an unfrequented coastline rolls out, with caves along its rocky shores and butterflies in plenty along the clifftop coastal heathland. The secluded shore runs all the way to Hopeman. This settlement follows the planned village pattern, and was founded as a fishing community in 1805, with a new harbour built in 1838 originally for exporting stone from local quarries.

Its near-neighbour Burghead is an altogether curious place – a grid-iron settlement laid out from 1805 onwards on the site of what was the largest Pictish fortress in Scotland, complete with three huge arrow-head shaped ramparts traversing the headland, their stone walls interlaced with nailed-together timbers. With little sentiment for the past, by the mid nineteenth century the town looked much as it does today. Burghead was an important fishing station as well as busy with exporting grain, and the granaries still survive around the harbour.

Moray becomes Highland (in an administrative sense) in the forests west of the bite of Findhorn Bay. Findhorn is a sleepy kind of place on the east side of the bay with its tidal sandflats. The treachery of tides has washed away the settlement at least twice in its long history. Long ago, Findhorn traded overseas with its own fleet, but the rise of Burghead finally finished off any economic importance, leaving the shingle and shifting sands for pleasure craft. Its name is now associated with the Findhorn Foundation, an international spiritual community with a transcendental and eco-friendly emphasis. The Culbin Forest, running westwards, has now tamed what was formerly the largest dune system in Britain. This previously sandy wasteland was created partly because of the persistent harvesting of marram grass for thatch in the seventeenth century. The removal of this stabilising plant loosened the dunes and a massive storm in 1694 overwhelmed the previously fertile fields and grazings. Clear of the trees by the endless shoreline, Culbin is still a lonely

place of shell-strewn beaches, white lines of distant surf, and a horizon filled with the hills across the Firth.

Returning to Lossiemouth and continuing east, there are other interesting habitats. The Lein is an odd, stony place, just to the east of Kingston on Spey, bounded by scrub and trees and mounded with water-smoothed stones. It is the largest shingle beach in Scotland and an important wildlife reserve. Kingston was named after Kingston-upon-Humber when it became the base of a shipbuilding industry, run by a Yorkshire-based company from 1784 onwards, but long vanished. Timber was floated down

SPEY BAY
On the skyline, Tugnet Ice House (1830) was once the largest salmon fishing station on the Spey, employing 150 people. The flat-bottomed fisher's boats in the foreground were used for casting salmon nets.

CULLEN
The sea-town area of Cullen predates by perhaps two centuries the planned town of 1820, which lies further up the hill.

A visitor centre, called the Buckie Drifter (named after a type of fishing vessel and a title probably mysterious to outsiders), tells the story of Buckie's now vanished herring fishery.

Two cheerful communities lie not far to the east, notably Findochty, with its brightly painted houses and neatly kept pleasure craft in a harbour swaying with masts and rigging. Here the art of decorating stonework by painting it in bright colours reaches its height. Some householders even have the mortar between the stonework obsessively picked out in a different colour – a tradition, it is said, which stems from the days when the exposure of these walls to the salty gales demanded tough oil-based paints to keep them in good condition. The pleasing effect can be seen again at the second settlement, Portknockie, with a pleasant clifftop coastal walk linking the two. Portknockie is also known for the Bow-fiddle Rock, a quartzite offshore stack whose resemblance to any musical instrument is tenuous.

The prettiest (arguably) of these Moray fishing communities is Cullen, again minutes to the east. Dominating the scene is a monument to the power and arrogance of the Seafield lairds. Though the railway has gone, the Cullen viaducts were built because the Great North of Scotland Railway was not permitted to

river from the upper reaches of the River Spey. This unlikely sounding activity lasted almost 100 years and nothing of it remains. Opposite Kingston stands Spey Bay, with another storm beach of grey pebbles, exposed and breezy. Look for leaping salmon, dolphins, seals, ospreys – sometimes happening all at once!

The coast swings round to Buckie and its satellite settlements such as Portgordon, its name recalling the ever-present Dukes of Gordon. The fourth Duke founded it in 1797. Buckie itself looks north, over the Firth, busy with its fishing and such ancillary industries.

cross Seafield policies and had to push its rails hard by the coast. Today, the arches tower above the old sea-town and frame sea views from the main street of the fine planned settlement of 1820. This handsome assembly of buildings around the main square replaced the old village of which only Cullen Kirk remains, near the former Seafield seat of Cullen House.

Apart from the attractions of the coast, many gain their first impression of Moray by way of the main A96 road between Aberdeen and Inverness. On this road is another important Moray town. Keith, formerly in the old county of Banffshire, still feels essentially Lowland in character and sits at the centre of a rich seam of farmland. Rebuilt by the Earl of Seafield in 1750, to replace the old settlement straggling along the banks of the River Isla, the Seafields employed the inevitable grid-plan, today skirted by the main road. An agricultural and manufacturing centre, Keith has for long been active with whisky and textiles. Strathisla Distillery (open to visitors) is one of the oldest in Scotland, while the Auld Brig, a packhorse bridge of 1609, once carried the main road north. (On the present main road, look for it in the dip, on the left past the supermarket.)

The A96 continues north-westward to descend to Fochabers. The Moray pattern of re-settlement occurs here as well: the former burgh of barony of 1598 was removed from its close proximity to Gordon Castle and rebuilt in the familiar grid and central square pattern by the fourth Duke of Gordon from 1776 onwards. As well as the food-processing of Baxters of Speyside there is a plant nursery, museum and a choice of walks including a short one to the Earth Pillars.

These are eroded sandstone pillars in the foreground of a fine view of the Spey south of the town. The Winding Walks signposted from the main road to the east are also worth exploring for a view through the trees and over the regular layout of Fochabers.

On the Inverness road towards the western edge of Moray, beyond Elgin, is the pleasing little town of Forres. Its Tolbooth (1838) and market cross (1844) have replaced their predecessors as reminders of the town's antiquity. (The royal charter was renewed by James IV in 1496.) The most spectacular Pictish work in Scotland is at the east end of the town. Sueno's Stone, of ninth-century origin and 23 ft (7 m) high, perhaps commemorates a victory of Pict over Dane. The Nelson Tower (1806) overlooking the town commemorates the famous admiral and offers wide panoramic views.

There are other excellent views from Cluny Hill,

STRATHISLA DISTILLERY
A typical single malt distillery, the oldest operating in the north, dating from 1786.

crofting township-turned-distillery centre. The highlight of a distillery visit here is Glen Grant, complete with attractive sheltered garden to explore. Nearby Craigellachie, built on the river terraces where the Fiddich meets the Spey, continues the distilling theme with its Speyside Cooperage. This visitor centre takes the theme of barrel making, a traditional craft vital to the whisky industry.

Also by Craigellachie is the handsome bridge over the Spey that carried the main road until 1972. Originally cast in Wales and brought by sea to Moray, this is reckoned to be the oldest iron span in Scotland, designed by Thomas Telford in 1814.

Close to Craigellachie, Dufftown, 'built on seven stills' is the classic whisky town, ringed by distilleries of which the best-known is Glenfiddich. The ruined Balvenie Castle, originally a thirteenth-century fortress, controlling the passes into lower Morayshire, sits on a wooden prominence above it – and lends its name to yet another malt whisky. Likewise in ruinous condition is Auchindoun Castle, overlooking the Fiddich from its own hilltop site near the town. The fortress was burned in 1592 in retaliation for the murder of the Bonnie Earl of Moray, of ballad fame.

CRAIGELLACHIE BRIDGE
Within 14 years of its completion, Craigellachie Bridge survived the worst flood ever recorded on the Spey in 1829.

another panoramic location to the south-east of Forres, where the Moray Firth stretches out to east and west. To the south of Forres, Randolph's Leap is a picturesque spot, where the River Findhorn is confined by rocks just narrow enough for a certain Alastair Cumming to have once leapt. He was retreating from a raid on Darnaway Castle and was hotly pursued by Thomas Randolph, Earl of Moray, the castle's owner. Rather unfairly it is the pursuer rather than the leaper whose name is recalled. Other attractions in the Forres area include Brodie Castle, in the care of the National Trust for Scotland, and home of the Brodie family since 1160.

Finally, turning north to the upper part of Morayshire, a string of whisky-distilling communities are worth exploring. These include Rothes, a former

Back on the River Spey, and a little way upstream from Craigellachie is the handsome and spacious Aberlour – more correctly Charlestown of Aberlour, recalling its foundation in 1812 by local laird Charles Grant. Riverside walks and a pleasing setting are among the community's attractions. Charles Grant took his precedent from his kinsman Sir Archibald Grant of Monymusk, who had founded Archiestown some 50 years previously, on a bare moor to the north-west of Aberlour.

Following the river south-eastwards, the main road runs by Ballindalloch Castle, dating from 1542, though later remodelled in baronial style. Near here is the confluence of the Avon with the Spey, the first already having joined with the River Livet. The land around the Livet belongs to the Glenlivet Estate, part of the Crown Estate since 1937. The whole amounts to 50,000 acres with farms, grouse moor, deer stalking and salmon beats – plus a network of waymarked trails.

Several roads lead on to Tomintoul, at 1150 ft (345 m) one of the highest villages in the north of Scotland. Tomintoul Museum tells the story of this village and its inevitable whisky connections. A road from the village leads on to the Lecht, on a route originally built as a military road in 1754. On the way

a curious four-square building stands in a hollow of the hills, visible from the main road. In this unlikely spot was an iron mine worked from 1730 onwards. The ore was carried by horses over to a spot near Nethybridge by the River Spey where sufficient timber was available to fuel the furnaces for smelting. This activity lasted only seven years, though the mine was reopened in 1841, this time for manganese – a venture started by the Duke of Gordon. Incredibly, a workforce of more than 60 laboured for five years, extracting the material and exporting it through the Duke's own harbour at Portgordon – a journey from the high ground of Moray, right down to the sea.

BALLINDALLOCH CASTLE
Home of the Macpherson Grants, Ballindalloch is exceptional in being privately owned and lived in continuously by the original family.

INDEX

Entries in **bold** indicate pictures

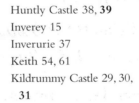

CRATHIE KIRK, near Balmoral Castle

This edition published by Colin Baxter Photography 2004
First published in Great Britain in 2000 by Lomond Books
Colin Baxter Photography Ltd., Grantown-on-Spey, Moray PH26 3NA

Photographs Copyright © Colin Baxter 2000, 2004
Text Copyright © Colin Baxter Photography Ltd 2000, 2004
All rights reserved

A CIP record for this book
is available from the British Library

ISBN 1-84107-229-X

Printed in China

Front cover photograph: RIVER DEE AT BALMORAL & DISTANT CAIRNGORMS
Page 1 photograph: BALMORAL CASTLE FROM THE AIR
Back cover photograph: THE VILLAGE OF CROVIE, GAMRIE BAY